What people are saying about Lessons at the Halfway Point:

Wally Amos,
Entrepreneur

Lessons is powerful work. Life is never really what it seems. It is always more. Have faith.

Father Leo Booth,
Author

An excellent book that stimulates our thoughts and behavior.

Dr. Joyce Brothers,
Author, Columnist

Making sense of the world we live in is what we should all be doing, but few of us take the time. Michael Levine's book is thought-provoking and helps lead us in a direction worth heading. It encourages us to grow. I found *Lessons* to be fascinating, courageous and original.

Marva N. Collins,
Educator

Lessons at the Halfway Point reminds me of the Thoreauvian quote that says: "I do not want to find that it is time to die and I never learned to live." *Lessons at the Halfway Point* reminds us daily to begin with the end in mind.

Bob Dole,
Senate Majority Leader

Those of us in politics need all the wisdom we can get, and Michael Levine has plenty of it.

Kathie Lee Gifford,
Talk-Show Hostess

Michael passes on wisdom beyond his years. You'll recognize yourself in this book and smile all the way through it.

Ben Gilberti,
The Wisdom Society

Exactly the kind of wisdom we look for "common sense is an uncommon degree" refreshing, piercing, disarming, enlightening, and practical.

J. Peter Grace,
Businessman/ Philanthropist

For the stressed-out business person with no time to read, these "lessons" are brief and to the point. They are also mind-expanding and consciousness-raising qualities essential for success in a fast-changing world.

Paul Harvey,
Syndicated Radio
Commentator

In the Missouri Ozarks, when anybody is able to reduce profound complexity to pithy, pertinent shirt-sleeved English — as Michael Levine does — it's said, "He has a gift for shucking right now to the cob." I'm glad Michael Levine labors on the side of propriety; he'd be a formidable adversary.

Charlton Heston,
Actor, Author

Michael Levine is the proprietor of an active and considering mind. I find myself agreeing with almost all of his observations in *Lessons at the Halfway Point* and chuckling at even more of them. Wry, dry, skeptical . . . and right.

Victor K. Kiam,
President, Remington
Products

The comments may be short and sweet, but the meaning runs very deep. You will recognize chickens that are brought home to roost.

Rabbi Harold
Kushner, *Author,*
When Bad Things
Happen to Good People

Some people can be wise, and some can be clever. Michael Levine is blessed with the ability to be both. His book is a real joy to read.

Frances Lear,
Editor, Lear's Magazine

Where were you when I was halfway? A terrific book.

Dr. Timothy Leary,
Author

. . . philosophic Home Runs.

Harvey Mackay,
Author, Swim With the
Sharks

. . . on a scale of 1–10 . . . a 12!

Father Michael
Manning,
Author

Not for the cowardly.

Lessons at the

Halfway Point

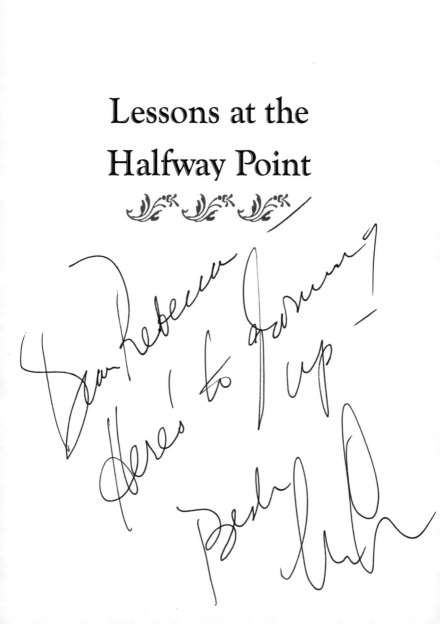

Lessons at the Halfway Point

Wisdom for Midlife

Michael Levine

CELESTIAL ARTS
Berkeley, California

Copyright © 1995 by Michael Levine. All rights reserved. No part of this
book may be reproduced in any form without the written permission of the
publisher, except in the case of brief quotations embodied in critical articles
or reviews.

CELESTIAL ARTS
P.O. Box 7123
Berkeley, California 94707

Please feel free to send your lessons at the halfway point to:
Michael Levine
c/o Aurora Publishing
433 N. Camden Dr.
Beverly Hills, CA 90210

Cover design by Fifth Street Design, Berkeley, California.
Text design and composition by Fifth Street Design.

Library of Congress Cataloging-in-Publication Data

Levine, Michael, 1954-
    Lessons at the halfway point / Michael Levine.
        p.   cm.
    ISBN 0-89087-744-0
    1. Middle age—Humor.   2. Middle age—Quotations, maxims, etc.
    I. Title.
    PN6231.M47L48   1995
    818' .5402—dc20   95-4026
                                                              CIP

FIRST PRINTING 1995

Printed in the United States of America
1 2 3 4 5 — 99 98 97 96 95

❧ CONTENTS ❧

❧ PREFACE ☙

"Our lives are brief beyond our comprehension or our desire,"
she told herself. "We drop like cotton with leaves from trees after
a single frost. The interval between birth and death is scarcely
more than a breathing space. Life is in the end nothing more than
a stirring of air, a shifting of life. No one of us, finally, can be
more than that. Even Einstein. Even Brahms."

From CONSIDER THIS SEÑORA
Harriet Doerr

s it dying, or coming to the end without having lived fully, that most frightens us?

A question at the halfway point, or perhaps *the* question.

The quote from Harriet Doerr makes the point gently, with poetry, a lullaby image — I even passed the duty to someone else — so you wouldn't kill the messenger. But, it has to be said. And this seemed more subtle than climbing a bell tower, screaming, "Time is limited. Death is real and restless. Peter Pan must grow up."

Statistically, I am at the halfway point. When my mind first (uncomfortably) settled on this idea, I felt a sense of panic about my mortality generally, but the time famine specifically. After a few weeks I settled down slightly, making moderate peace with the fact that we are, in the words of poet Carl Sandburg, "all riding on a limited express."

What helped me relax a bit was to focus on some of my lessons so far.

Introductions are supposed to explain the Who, What, and Why's. Well, the resulting doubt and concern and confusion is the reason I, for four years, wrote this book.

I composed these lessons incessantly. I tried to stop a couple of times but they haunted me. Just when I thought there were no more, more would come, usually in the lonely cool before dawn.

Turning 40. Hot baths. A Nap. A week or so, worthy of a Guinness nomination under world's record for using the phrase "Why bother?" Questions that wouldn't rest. Answers that present hope though didn't rhyme.

And then serendipitously, I read an old Scout training book about what to do when you're lost. "Stop. Investigate. Go over everything you know. And if you move. Leave a note."

This book is my note.

The first realization was the desultory way we live. So little focus on direction. Laggard on even the most obvious problems in our lives. When I slowed enough to look carefully, I watched people everyday make decisions, often unconsciously, to live their life in the next 24 hours as an angel or an insect. And the more I watched the more I learned — quickly realizing that when you learn something about yourself or the world you are ripe for a celebration. For to explain human nature is not to defend it.

Impressions flood forth: We are becoming richer and richer in technology, poorer and poorer in meaning. The basic need to fuse with another to transcend the prison of separateness is closely related to that other human desire — knowing the secret of man. Thinking is the hardest work there is, which is probably why so few engage in it. We have an ethical duty to pay attention, resist easy temptation and distraction, and accept responsibility for what we do, whether as individuals or as a society. Growing older has a palliative effect on most young people's rage. There is no escaping the shadowed side of human behavior and its propensity to sin. Examination of the outer world is not nearly as painful as exploration of the inner sphere. As we begin to understand who we are, and why we are who we are, we uniquely negotiate the obstacle course called life. We naturally try to escape pain by dulling the nerve endings of our souls and when we are hurting, nothing matters more than finding relief. Anyone who takes their destiny as a human being seriously has struggled with these problems and more. These questions and how to respond to them are the essence of what it means to be authentically human.

Without explanation, I began keeping a journal. Why? To print up as a gift for my friends on my fortieth birthday, as a way of saying, "thank you for staying with me." I was going through the usual feelings, aches, pains, and bruises to the soul leading to the mantra: "Nobody's ever felt like this before." I felt occasionally self-absorbed, but found comfort in action. Contentment in writing the lessons, I began to feel more peaceful. This became most clear one day when in my desire to scream and yell, I recognized, "Isn't that what hell is for?"

An accumulation of thoughts, a collection of lessons. Things I've bumped into. Tripped over. Clipped out. Learned. And been forced to learn, compelled to discover. Life is like that.

Discoveries big and small. Ideas that rang and still ring. A glimpse that caught my eye. Wisdom picked up at parties. Spittoon philosophy. And some conclusions so obvious. Oh, yes, so obvious.

On the day I finished the book, I walked outside my house plagued with separation anxiety for a constant friend for the last four years. It was hot outside, 108°F with I-miss-the-rain-forest-style humidity. I passed my eighty-three-year-old neighbor who is leaning on his cane, pushing his fish cap jauntily, and I shout, "howyadoing?"

His reply? "Best day, yet!"

I immediately decided to stand straighter. For posture, like attitude, is important.

Now there are parts of this book, I understand, that might as well come with a fuse and matches but it was my intention that these lessons at the halfway point will both comfort the afflicted while afflicting the comfortable.

They did for me.

Life

Goes On...

We often stay in Hell a very long time because we know
the names of the streets.

☙

You can dance alone, but it's a lonely dance.

☙

You cannot be interdependent until you
are first independent.

☙

*Nothing is as stressful as trying to be a different person than
who you are.*

☙

Fear and pain are the gasoline that fuels the engine
of psychological change.

☙

Often tragically, we respond to light as if it were darkness, and to darkness as if it were light.

❦

When you stop spending time with your real friends, you lose your balance.

❦

Generally, people change because they have to.

❦

People evaluate intelligence much more leniently than morality. That's because most people understand that even intelligent people do really stupid things.

❦

Amazingly, people think that the things that happen to them only happen to them.

❦

We realize our potential only by leaving Eden. We mature only by realizing that childhood is over. Attempts to stay or return to the womb cut off our human potential.

❦

There is no shortcut through the firewalk.

❦

More people in America are starving for love than for food.

❦

Human nature is tribal.

❦

Things that happen immediately are more graphic than things that happen down the line. So, a child fears the pain of a hypodermic needle, thinking little of a lifetime without polio.

Integration doesn't mean standing shoulder to shoulder, it means standing heart to heart.

Our principles are a reflection of our self-image.

Some of us laugh when we need to cry.

Certain sad people are so detached from themselves that they actually hurt themselves as a way to feel something . . . anything. Their marked withdrawal from reality borders on autism.

Angry people all have one thing in common: they lack gratitude.

It's occurred to me that the lies we tell ourselves are much more pernicious than the lies we tell others. "I'm nothing like my mother" . . . "I'm too busy to exercise" . . . "Sex isn't that important" . . . "I don't need therapy" . . . "I don't want to get married."

As you look at history, it becomes apparent that human behavior is much easier to predict than the weather.

Narcissists tend toward human warmth that would
make Frigidaire proud.

❦

Chaos is often what people fear most.

❦

People who feel their internal world is out of control often try
to control their outside world by becoming very orderly.

❦

*It seems to me that in most human capacities, the less we use it, the
less we see it as worth using.*

❦

People with an absence of passion and enthusiasm are
in real trouble.

❦

*People act differently when they own things. When was the last time
you took a rental car to the car wash before returning it?*

❦

The only way of being an authentically sacred person is
through constant, uncensored questioning of yourself.

❦

Lots of people make promises. Few make commitments.

❦

The moral credibility of any group or person comes
overwhelmingly from their ability to criticize themselves.

❦

Saying "I forgive you" isn't hard. But meaning it is.

❦

Effort matters in everything, love included. Learning to love is purposeful work.

❦

Most people prefer demonstrations of love to declarations of it.

❦

Cliques are a verdant garden for growing an ample supply of paranoid xenophobics with hurricane force.

❦

Because most people value human survival above all else, the prospect of being hanged concentrates the mind like little else can.

❦

It is true that some desperate people do desperate things. But it is also true that some non-desperate people do desperate things.

❦

Forgiveness of self is where all forgiveness starts.

❦

Some people need to be more patient, and some people need to be less patient.

❦

When people betray themselves, their excuses wash up on the shore in unrecognizable pieces.

❦

People who are tentative about making plans are often unsure
of their ability to show up.

❦

People who look like gangsters often act like them.

❦

People who don't love themselves do not think they deserve to
be loved. Ironically, they hear compliments as if
they were criticisms.

❦

*If you've ever dreamed of having sex with a co-worker, don't feel bad
. . . most people have.*

❦

If you don't defend your honor, people will assume
you have none.

❦

Millions of people can be wrong.

❦

Fans who go too far become fanatics.

❦

No fanatic considers themself a fanatic.

❦

What some people lack in talent they make up in ego.

❦

It is the trivial that looms largest among the self-absorbed.

❦

Sometimes we don't like our best teachers.

❦

To change someone's mind, you must speak to their heart and listen. Beliefs are generally a matter of faith — not logic.

❦

The direct route to knowledge is experience.

❦

Changed lives are changed from the inside out.

❦

While working to increase self-control, begin with small steps until your sense of honor becomes greater than your impulses and moods.

❦

Although some conflicts can't be settled, at the very least, trying to solve them (even if unsuccessfully) promotes personal growth.

❦

As children, we shudder in the dark. The concealed troubles us. But ironically, as we grow up, it is our destiny to live in the twilight.

❦

Growth responds to willingness.

❦

Time likes to play nasty little jokes as the years pass. The cruelest one of all is that you find yourself upholding values you once thought foul, and rejecting ideas you once held close to your soul.

❦

Often people injured by loss of love in their childhood spend the rest of their adult lives insatiably pursuing collections of things, often at the cost of human relationships.

When life serves up tragedy, it is your decision whether to participate in an autopsy or a revivification.

To be more interesting demands being more interested.

You will feel no stability in the outer world until you feel it internally.

It is vital to give yourself credit for the agony you have survived throughout your life.

To live happily in the age of self-improvement, it is critical to know the limits of what is possible.

Sometimes even the most competent people respond to stress in an infantile manner.

Prefer evolution to revolution.

It is impossible to really love someone until you really know them; therefore, the obligation to love your neighbor begins with knowing your neighbor. Only through that conscious decision will you begin to

approach the solution to life's most difficult challenge —
loving the stranger.

❧

Share in the pain of others instead of instantly trying to ease it.
It is in communion that we learn the shape of anguish and
identify its shadows when it passes through our own lives.

❧

One indicator of middle age is the sudden attraction to naps.

❧

Our obstacles are as dear to us as our struggle to be
free of them.

❧

The pursuit of the inner child has taken over just when Americans
ought to be thinking more about the outer adult.

❧

Tragic events need not ruin our lives. They bear the seeds of
transformational healing and spiritual awakening if we only are
willing to receive them.

❧

If you don't get angry at people who deserve your anger, you will get
angry at those who don't deserve your anger.

❧

Life is a game of inches.

❧

If we don't pursue our "correct calling," we rot.

❧

You can't be happy in life by avoiding risks or action. While seated on the bench, football players are safe and secure, but miserable. They plead with the coach to get in the game. Once out there on the field, they are tackled time after time. They are left battered and bruised . . . but happy.

❦

Very much like human eruptions, earthquakes have been shown to be not abrupt unforeseen occurrences at all, but rather the products of years of inaudible strain.

❦

Excuse-making has been a natural tendency ever since Adam blamed Eve, and Eve blamed the serpent.

❦

The secret to life is that there is no secret to life. It's just hard work.

❦

People who think they will find lasting happiness in things may be nice people, but they're fools.

❦

For an old idea to die and a new and better idea to take its place, one must go through a period of confusion.

❦

You can't slay all the dragons at once . . . and there is no dishonor in slaying them one at a time.

❦

Everyone should develop their very own Personal Accomplishments list, noting the things that they are most proud of achieving, and should look at it several times a year. It's especially comforting when you're feeling down.

❦

Extraordinary people are most often ordinary people
with extraordinary determination.

❦

We teach what we need to learn, and we write what we need to know.

❦

Reflect on how your childhood is affecting your life now.

❦

*Is it possible that the journey into real adulthood begins with the
understanding that human existence is limited?*

❦

Unfortunately, people can't learn how to trust. All they can do
is put themselves in situations with trustworthy people. It's the
experience of being in a trustworthy situation that changes the
way you view the world.

❦

*Many important battles in life have to be fought more than once
to be won.*

❦

A wise friend told me, "I ain't where I ought to be and I ain't
where I'm gonna be, but I ain't where I was, either." Me, too.

❦

*People need encouragement to live. Without it, people begin the
process of dying — slowly and sadly.*

❦

To be conscious is to develop and to develop is
to occasionally despair.

❦

*By spotlighting your immediate needs, you can lose your ultimate
goals. Center on your life's primary mission, your most profound
dreams, your most beautiful hopes.*

❦

A person's inquisitive quotient has always appealed to me more
than their intelligence quotient.

❦

*No athlete, no artist, no president fulfills all of their dreams. A
successful person's reach always exceeds their grasp.*

❦

Many people are experts at wasting time.

❦

Tranquility exists halfway between insufficiency and excess.

❦

Victims spend their time making sure that everybody knows it's
somebody else's fault.

❦

It is useless to search for what is already gone.

❦

You can't fence the world out, without fencing yourself in.

❦

If you receive rewards you didn't earn, you are a candidate for depression.

We must train ourselves not to see the world only through our own eyes.

At some point, you have to stop reading, stop talking, stop studying, and do it.

The first step toward real clarity is confusion.

Without struggle there is no progress.

Fame without achievement is worthless and is ultimately a source of torture to the hero.

Consciousness is both the source of our agony and the root of our salvation.

Home

Front...

Having children makes you no more a parent than having a piano at home makes you a pianist.

❦

Just as a religious person must account for the child born with deformities, so the atheist must account for children being born at all.

❦

Though many ads pitch to young people driving cars in tight jeans, it's the silver-haired ones in the loose-fitting pants that usually do most of the buying.

❦

Policemen often notice that not only do the young men they arrest not have a responsible male in the house, they've often never met one.

❦

Don't despair. Tough love is tough.

❦

Didn't it make you mad the first time you found out that your dad was letting you win at checkers?

❦

I wonder how many parents have ever asked the question, "Can I divorce my child?"

❦

Remember when the only things kids in school had to dodge were spitballs?

❦

Parents should consciously commit themselves to finding out who their children really are before they worry about what they might become.

❦

We have been raised as consumers. If something doesn't work, we throw it away and get a new one. Well, it's the same thing with couples. If our partner doesn't change or conform to our expectations, we get rid of them.

❦

I favor national service for all eighteen-year-olds for many reasons, not the least of which is that it acts as a powerful reminder of our sense of responsibilty to society.

❦

Anyone who says that truth is stranger than fiction has never heard a young person explain why they arrived home an hour past their curfew.

❦

Three things that all children must know: Who's the boss . . .
what the rules are . . . and who is going to enforce them.

*Like it or not, I've had to confront my increasing age when I describe the
music listened to by today's teenagers as "the musical version of the flu."*

If I could only do one thing to improve education in America,
I think it would be to institute a dress code.

*If I could do a second thing, it would be to demand a minimum of a C
grade for a driver's license at the age of sixteen.*

Can anyone argue that parents who smoked pot with their
children in the '60s and '70s don't owe them an apology?

*Children who watch television all afternoon, all night, and all
weekend, will go down in history . . . not to mention arithmetic,
geography, and science.*

I read with interest not long ago that Maine has the lowest
personal expenditure in the nation and the highest SAT scores.
This leads me to suggest a vast new program for American
education that will cost nothing. The program is called:
Homework!

The greatest humiliation of all is being unloved as a child.

Advantaged children often turn out to
be not-so-advantaged adults.

❦

*My hometown of Los Angeles is the currently handing out condoms to
high school students. Hopefully, handing out education will not be
too far behind.*

❦

The next time someone starts talking about the good old days,
remind them that in 1920 toilet paper was a luxury and that
only half of all homes in America had toilets at all.

❦

*Remember when most parents would have been thrilled if their
daughter married a lawyer?*

❦

Single fathers are capable of being good fathers, but never good
mothers, and vice versa.

❦

*Historically, a man has learned masculinity primarily from his father.
Today, many boys are drifting into a dangerous hyper-masculinity,
constantly overcompensating for their lack of a true role model.*

❦

Trust me, I've been to some family get-togethers that were
more hostile than the MacLaughlin group.

❦

Some people are more loving, attentive grandparents than parents.

❦

Responsible parents today are parenting in spite of
the popular culture.

*Parents who brag about their children quoting Socrates at age two
should be slapped about the head and face.*

Work before play, children before parents.

Live your life in the manner that you would like your kids to live theirs.

The odds are stacked against children born to single mothers.
All too often, material, emotional, and spiritual poverty is all
they ever inherit.

*Unfortunately, the family has been playing without a clear set of rules
for the better part of a generation.*

If a parent has not taught his child that life is difficult, he has
cursed the child.

*Children living in homes with no one to turn to for love and protection
are living as the hostages.*

Almost no one makes plans for the inevitability of becoming
their parents' "parent."

If parents love their children, they should raise them so that other people can as well.

❦

The more people learn about the details of their parents' lives, the more they may be forced to recognize how much they resemble them.

❦

You're probably too overprotective a parent if all the other parents you know are too permissive.

❦

Set aside ten minutes for yourself as quiet time to put the work day behind you before you try to leap into the loving father/mother husband/wife routine.

❦

If you've not been loved well as a child, it is often very difficult to love yourself.

❦

Whenever I'm in a public setting, I am astounded at how few parents insist that their children say "please" and "thank you."

❦

The black families in America are in big trouble. The idea that government interaction can stop the hemorrhage is nuttier than a squirrel's breakfast. The truth is that if black children are are going to be saved, their parents have to do more to help themselves.

❦

The single most important thing I learned about step-parenting is to lower your expectations. Let the child come to you.

🍦

The central mission of parenting is to prepare your children to be independent from you. By sheltering them from the realities of the world, in an effort to be kind you end up being cruel.

🍦

What happened to the word, let alone the concept, of "chores" for kids?

🍦

The truth is that most Americans feel strongly that intentional single parenthood is a problem that should not be celebrated, but rather solved.

🍦

You've been home with the kids too long when you watch a wedding between two puppets on "Mr. Rogers" and start to cry.

🍦

Letter writing can be very therapeutic. It gives you a chance to organize what you want to say and gives the recipient a chance to read your words more than once and reflect on them.

🍦

Adolescent stress is a cultural, not biological phenomenon.

🍦

The loss of some friends is actually no loss at all.

🍦

Mad

about You...

Women yearn for a man and men yearn for women.

❦

Men don't want to date men with breasts.

❦

I used to think prenuptial agreements were
horrible documents.

❦

*Women who accept large, inappropriate gifts from men are
working, and if they don't know that, they are even more pathetic.*

❦

Those who have loved the truly troubled know intimately
the definition of the term "no-win situation." Your
concern is perceived as lack of trust and your discretion as
lack of interest.

❦

Men who avoid intimacy are doomed to immaturity and isolation.

❁

I wonder if I have crossed the minds of women with whom I've shared love, as they have mine.

❁

Men look at the world through a window and women look at the world through a mirror.

❁

Scientists are now fascinated at how close the human reproductive strategies have come to look more like those of the birds and bees than anyone could have imagined.

❁

It would seem a good idea not to look at engagements as merely a prelude to bliss, but a time of working out nitty-gritty personal issues before the most serious commitment of your life.

❁

The pounding of your heart in romance and the pounding of your heart in danger are perhaps the same thing.

❁

Those who resist believing that men and women are different should consider that only one group wears uncomfortable shoes because they look good in them.

❁

Relationships you thought existed only in dreams, do.

❁

The war between the sexes has become an ambiguous series of skirmishes and sorties.

Relationships can be as addicting as drugs and alcohol, with just as painful withdrawals.

The first casualty of divorce is trust.

Many women have mistaken coldness for strength of character.

You can visit every bookstore and library in the world and never find a book titled How to Get Her to Commit.

Many people find it easier to have sex than to talk about it.

Do you think that if the Titanic sank today, male passengers would refuse to enter lifeboats because they weren't sure if women remained on board?

People often think most obsessively about past relationships that were conducted on the sly.

Before you focus on finding the right person, concentrate on being the right person.

Women would do well to initiate lovemaking more often.

❦

Bravery, control, resolution, and honor can make a person very attractive.

❦

Kissing fulfills important psychological needs: touching, intimacy, and communication.

❦

The essence of love begins when infatuation ends.

❦

The idea that people can charge others with sexual harassment, offering no more evidence that they said "pass the coffee" voluptuously with a grin on their face, is sad news for everyone.

❦

Embarking on an impulse marriage is like buying a car without a road test, though the consequences can, by far, be worse.

❦

An award-winning film director told me that ninety percent of a good movie is casting. I wonder if it is also true with a successful marriage.

❦

When you're engaged in a relationship of foolishness, it squeezes out any room for real loving.

❦

Today it's easier to walk away from a marriage than from an agreement to purchase a used car.

❦

Females are more in tune with their physical selves, which brings them more in touch with their emotions, since our emotions reside in our bodies not in our minds.

Seldom does anything feel close to the first night together.

It isn't the disparity between two people in a relationship that produces difficulty, but instead the way these conflicts are dealt with when they occur.

Although males and females do not battle with the same weapons, they withstand the same injuries.

Friendships are good training for the intimacy you desire in romantic relationships.

Even the smallest personal alterations may cause large variations within a relationship.

A new relationship should take work . . . but how much work?

Even people who live the quietest, most mundane lives fortunately have the capacity for robust sensuality.

The way in which people experience their sense of self mirrors the way they develop intimate relationships.

You cannot achieve intimacy until you stop viewing others as an extension of yourself.

❧

Infatuation is instant desire. It's one set of glands calling to another. It isn't love.

❧

Romantic love is a contradiction filled with a deep need to connect and an irrational fear of connection.

❧

Letting your lover know you understand them is the most powerful tool in healing a relationship.

❧

Marrying in hopes of avoiding conflict and loneliness is like jumping in a lake to avoid getting wet.

❧

Involvement in a relationship with a troubled person often feels similar to being a victim of a drive-by shooting.

❧

Some men spend more time maintaining their lawn than they do their relationships.

❧

A married person can be (and often is) more involved in an affair without sexual contact than the physical variety. This relationship, often defined by sneaking around, is an unholy alliance, and is as loathsome as an ulcer to the heart of a relationship. In some ways, this type of affair is worse than the more carnal brand.

❧

Love doesn't have to feel dizzying.

*There have been times in my life when I wished love would
leave me alone.*

Many people believe that loving someone is supposed to take
the pain of their life away and, often, it ends up doing
just the opposite.

*The difference in the way men and women shop: men go in knowing
what they want and women often go in to relax.*

Authors of obituaries perceive the sexes very differently. Men
are described as "intelligent," "experienced entrepreneurs," while
women are "faithful," "likeable," "adorable."

*From a lifetime of reading obituaries, it seems that husbands tend to
kill wives because of wounded egos, and wives tend to kill husbands
because of battered bodies.*

Parenthood undeniably reshapes a marriage, sometimes for the
better, sometimes for the worse.

*There is a serious debate within the scientific community about the
possibility of a hereditary component to sexual orientation. If we reach*

*a point where this becomes provable, it will completely rewrite
dialogue on the subject in a way nothing else has or ever could.*

❧

When women say "men are pigs," they're not altogether off the
mark. The male nature is animal-like, and women would do
well to both make peace with that and understand their unique
ability to humanize it.

❧

*Most people see their ex-husbands or ex-wives with either
rose-colored or manure-colored glasses, but seldom accurately.*

❧

If you only thought about it logically, you'd never allow
yourself to fall in love again or be part of a true friendship.

❧

*As an exercise, to illustrate its impossible mystery, take a big piece of
paper and try to write a simple definition of love.*

❧

I have met a few women (not many) that seriously consider
their shoe salesperson more important to them than their
doctor, dentist, or clergyman.

❧

*The more you need romance in your life, the less likely you are to have
it; the less you need it, the more likely you are to have it.*

❧

The other day I saw a woman driving with a license plate
marked "PMS" — I immediately changed lanes.

❧

After divorce, most people are understandably as suspicious as a rich widow.

🌱

I am now absolutely convinced that men don't understand, in the deepest sense, what the subject of eating or food means for women. In the same way, women don't understand the issue of sexual variety for men.

🌱

I gag (so to speak) with sadness at the thought of the millions of women mutilating themselves in the bulimia tragedy.

🌱

Based on a casual survey I did of singles ads in the classifieds, most people consider smoking less attractive than malaria.

🌱

It is very easy for women to manipulate men. Men are not that evolved.

🌱

When somebody loves you for what you are and you hate yourself, you hate that person for loving you.

🌱

Men who are obsessed with a beautiful woman first find themselves dazzled, then fascinated, then blinded, and, ultimately, enslaved.

🌱

Sometimes love just sneaks up on you.

🌱

As a romance ends, women don't hurt more than men, just differently.

🌱

A moment gone, is gone forever, like water through your hands.

Men don't understand the pressures on women physically in the same way that women don't understand the pressure on men financially.

Men who first marry late in life are weak marriage material.

Men really appreciate women who overlook their mistakes.

Too bad sex is seldom like in the movies.

For men, sexual rejection is total rejection.

It seems to me that by the time they reach adolescence, an enormous number of girls experience a dramatic loss of self-esteem emerging into adulthood with much less confidence than their male counterparts.

Every relationship takes up where the last one left off.

For women, femininity plus sensuality equals magic.

What we keep secret is the key to our identity.

You love that which you devote your time and attention to.

If a man talks dirty to a woman, its sexual harassment. If a woman talks dirty to a man, it's $2.98 a minute.

☙

Why do so many women with fake fingernails, eyelashes and breasts, complain that there are no real men.

☙

How about a new Barbie divorcee doll? It could come with all of Ken's stuff.

☙

Marrying someone you don't know well is like playing Russian Roulette — only worse.

☙

Postcards

from the Edge...

Parachute makers make better parachutes when they are randomly forced to test them.

❦

I dare you to ask a stranger in an elevator, "What is your least favorite planet?"

❦

Don't expect more than a grunt from a pig.

❦

Too bad you can't claim people who are codependant as deductions on your income tax.

❦

Lucky for Noah, it wasn't raining when he started building the ark.

❦

A pat on the back is only eighteen inches from a kick in the ass.

❦

The other day, a friend introduced me to a stockbroker named John. He said, "Call me Jack for short." Just how much shorter is that?

❦

When you play New Age music backwards, you get New Age music.

❦

Definition of a codependent: you blow up and I go to pieces.

❦

Just for fun sometime, call up a porno theater and ask for the feature film's plot.

❦

Happy-faced optimists say that the world is moving quickly in the direction of sanity, but the popularity of professional wrestling tells a different story.

❦

The weirdest dare I ever turned down involved nutty friends challenging me to write to the President of McDonald's to find out if Ronald McDonald is gay.

❦

Pessimism wilts everything around it.

❦

Beware of health clubs that resemble live versions of the Playboy Channel.

❦

People don't learn when they're defensive.

❦

Perception of the same object can be quite different, depending on whether you are remembering or imagining it.

❦

Hotel room service: It's like eating in an expensive restaurant in which the decor is unmade beds and clothes hung over the chairs.

❦

People who are critical of others should be deeply critical of themselves.

❦

In most areas of life, the trophy will go to the curious.

❦

There's a big difference between wanting to be big and wanting big things.

❦

The pursuit of perfection often impedes improvement.

❦

While it's true that you can tell a lot about someone's character from their friends, the same is true about their enemies.

❦

A year is shorter to a person who is sixty than to one who is ten, because a year to a person who is ten is one-tenth of their life, while to a person who's sixty, it's one-sixtieth.

❦

One of the great mistakes is the refusal to set aside trivia.

❦

There is often no reward for taking a courageous stand.

❦

Most of life is timing.

❦

If people eat garbage, they must regard themselves on some level as a trash bin.

❦

Please remember that when you are kind to the cruel you end up being cruel to the kind.

❦

If you sell most of your things, you purchase liberty.

❦

Mysteries can't be solved by merely repeating the question.

❦

Living with someone doesn't ensure intimacy.

❦

Most confrontations are efforts to avert the true argument.

❦

Although the egocentric seem infatuated with themselves and unable to care for others, they are actually not capable of real self-love, either.

❦

The weak fear the strong because they expose their weakness.

❦

"Childish" and "childlike" are not the same thing.

❦

Having a birthday next to a major holiday makes
you feel robbed.

❦

The anticipation of a dreaded event is often worse than the event itself.

❦

Often, the way we see a problem is the problem.

❦

Before you can tell the truth, you have to know what it is.

❦

If you were a captive tiger, it seems like a circus would be a
more stimulating home than a zoo.

❦

A sign of decline: Your memories exceed your dreams.

❦

There are no squabbles in the world like those between sisters
over clothes or French restaurants over cuisine.

❦

If you have a "why," you can deal with almost any "what."

❦

History is clear when you look back, but messy when you're
going through it.

❦

With some people, getting a word in edgewise is like trying to sneak the sun past a rooster.

❦

Looking from any sixth-floor window will show you that Oswald had a tough shot at a moving target.

❦

Those who are not honest about internal conflicts engage in external ones. They create drama because silence is deafening and peace and quiet are terrifying.

❦

The two primary reasons people fail are irresponsibility and fear.

❦

More time should be spent researching the practical than exploring the bizarre.

❦

The endless parade of whining, shrill complainers on television talk shows are beginning to sound a great deal like a chorus of gerbils caught underneath a doorjamb.

❦

Can you believe some of the things that people try to justify as carry-on luggage on airplanes¿

❦

Pacifists would do well to remember that it was tanks — not words, not prayers, not negotiations — that liberated the concentration camps.

❦

Not all monsters are make-believe.

❦

Depression is anger turned inward.

❦

The reason that editors rather than reporters are responsible for creating newspaper headlines is that most people aren't good at summing up their own work.

❦

Aiming is not hitting. Meaning well is not necessarily doing well.

❦

Silence is agreement.

❦

The back of a Lay's potato chip bag has more words on it than the Gettysburg Address.

❦

If you beat a dog you know where the dog won't be, and if you feed a dog you know where the dog will be.

❦

Truth is like ammonia on a dirty windshield.

❦

There are ripple effects from a life of hypocrisy.

❦

Freud was right: "Sometimes a cigar is just a cigar."

❦

The opposite of pride is shame. The opposite of love and hate is indifference.

❦

Commandments without a commander have no worth.

❦

Articulate bigotry is still bigotry.

❦

If you desire freedom from all obligations, you will never really be free.

❦

Courage isn't the absence of fear. It is taking action in the presence of fear.

❦

There's no accountability without punishment.

❦

Living in the closet is like living in a coffin. But at least in the coffin you're lying down.

❦

It's harder to debunk a false charge than to make it.

❦

No one should be permitted to start intricate conversations and then go to sleep.

❦

You are always an ambassador for someone or something.

❦

Most learning occurs outside of schools.

❦

Relationships are assignments.

❦

We do the world a real service when we conduct ourselves as adults, assume others to perform as adults, and treat them as adults.

❦

To be a leader, you have to start leading.

❦

The names you are called don't matter. Only the names to which you respond matter.

❦

Remember that conviction is contagious.

❦

You cannot forgive anyone with whom you've never gotten angry.

❦

Things that we become obsessive and compulsive about are those we believe are capable of taking away our despair.

❦

If people stopped tipping mediocre service in restaurants, I have a sneaking suspicion it would improve pretty fast.

❦

Isn't it amazing that our nation has thousands of citizens volunteering for starvation?

❦

Writing a eulogy to someone beloved is infinitely harder than to someone not personally known.

❦

Dividing history into decades is an understandable exercise in trying to package the unpackagable.

❦

Because radio is something we typically listen to while doing something else, we tend not to take it as seriously as other media.

❦

Accepting responsibility for someone else's happiness is a lot trickier than being responsible for their unhappiness.

❦

A great deal can be learned from scrutinizing the familiar.

❦

Through the use of enough force, it is possible to hammer a square peg into a round hole. But in the process, it gets frayed around the edges.

❦

The voices of extraordinary writers are almost as quickly recognizable as those of great singers.

❦

There are better stories on the placemats at Burger King than in the lyrics of most country-western songs.

❦

There's no such thing as one ideal image anymore. Reality is much more complex, and much more interesting.

❦

I've always found it fascinating that the suicide rate of handicapped people is far less than those not handicapped.

❦

The majority of overweight people I know skip breakfast and the majority of thin people don't.

❦

Having it all was the big lie of our time.

❦

With excess comes arrogance. With arrogance comes excess.

❦

I think it's important to remember that the winners write the history books.

❦

At pivotal points in history, it is the towering presence of an individual more than any other factor, that determines the turn of events rather than an idea or movement. At other times, the absence of a strong personality has had a reverse effect.

❦

Cynicism born of hindsight is easy. Cynicism born of experience is sad. Cynicism born of arrogance in pathetic.

❦

A person who speaks is more powerful than thousands who are silent.

❦

It's easy to be tolerant if you stand for nothing.

❦

Flossing in public takes guts.

🎋

When I think about most modern innovations, their necessity seems so obvious in hindsight.

🎋

I think a good sign that you might be overusing your credit card is if you hide the bill from your spouse until a "good time."

🎋

What you don't release, you pass on.

🎋

Bruce Springsteen has mellowed, sounding unmistakably like a man who has changed some diapers.

🎋

It takes a secure man to wear plaid.

🎋

Modern American culture looks strangely like the one that led to the fall of the Roman Empire.

🎋

When I was growing up, I heard that two can live as cheaply as one. Whoever said that didn't own a calculator.

🎋

There's a difference between a gift and a present. A present is something you are giving the receiver because it's something you want them to have. A gift is something that you know the receiver wants.

🎋

It takes courage, strength, and humility to enter psychological therapy in order to face fear, weakness, and pride.

❦

Bad things come not only from idle hands but also from inactive minds.

❦

Ever since I stopped shaking hands and hugging people with runny noses, the number of colds I've gotten has dropped dramatically.

❦

People in my life who have a less-than-average fear of death also have a less-than-average fear of life.

❦

It seems that the more responsibility that people have on their shoulders, the less room they have for chips.

❦

People who have sloppy cars have sloppy lives.

❦

From the top of the hill you are permitted to reveal the ways in which you have felt excluded, ashamed, or generally out of it. From the bottom of the hill no one seems to care.

❦

I'm sorry, but some rap artists sound like my kitchen disposal with a fork caught in it.

❦

My three favorite lies are: 1. Go ahead and tell me, I promise I won't get mad. 2. I'll do it in a minute. 3. The doctor will call you right back.

❦

Amazing: Mickey Mouse is approaching social security age.

❦

Sometimes there's nothing wrong with the brakes; they're just applied too late.

❦

When questioned about what he predicted as the terminus of civilization's degeneracy, T. S. Eliot visualized people casually shooting each other. At the time he was laughed at and dismissed as an alarmist.

❦

What most people think of air travel today is best evidenced by the speed with which they want to exit the plane when it lands.

❦

Little could be worse than waking up during surgery.

❦

With success comes arrogance.

❦

You can't start a fire without a spark.

❦

There are fifty ways to leave your lover, but only six exits from the airplane.

❦

Is it me, or has Christmas and New Years Day become essentially an excuse for people to take a powder at work starting mid-Novemeber?

❦

Why is it that women who have a weight problem often have a great shoe collection?

❦

Television comercials have truly become an insomniac's late night field of dreams.

❦

Language is funny. There is no difference in the meaning between "fat chance" and "slim chance."

❦

Wheel

of Fortune...

Successful people are very lucky. Just ask any failure.

🍸

Expecting nothing bad to happen to you because you're a good person is like expecting a bull not to charge you because you're a vegetarian.

🍸

Often, people who don't work are more exhausted than people who do.

🍸

The uncreative mind can spot the wrong answer, but it takes a creative mind to spot the wrong question.

🍸

With the death of Communism, why aren't more people celebrating the triumph of capitalism?

🍸

Honesty, confidence, and talent to inspire are the values at the core of effective leadership.

❦

It is only the strongest leaders who have the confidence to employ the most qualified people possible, without fear of being overshadowed.

❦

Any job can be made great. It's the worker — not the work — that counts.

❦

The most successful cultures regard private business ownership almost as moral obligation.

❦

It's better to be 0 for 20 than 0 for 0.

❦

Balancing your budget is like protecting your virtue. You have to learn to say No.

❦

The first rule of money management is knowing what you've got. The second is knowing what you want.

❦

Successful people demonstrate consistency between words and actions.

❦

Happiness tends to drop in unexpectedly when you are working hard on something meaningful.

❦

Business owners should remember that old customers spend
more, refer new customers, and cost less to do business with
than new customers.

❦

*Some people's economic view is more animated by a desire to hurt the
wealthy than it is to help the poor.*

❦

It doesn't surprise me that hyperactive children are four times
more likely than their peers to grow up and start a business.

❦

*Businesses should hire for attitude and train for skill. It's easier to
teach someone how to work a cash register than it is to teach them
how to smile.*

❦

Telling champions to give up is like telling water
to run upstream.

❦

You know you're doing something right when you start being copied.

❦

A pessimist is someone who complains about the noise
when opportunity knocks.

❦

*The job of a manager is not to do everything — it is to make sure that
every task gets done.*

❦

What hurts most businesses is a lack of fortitude.

❦

What self-help books and business manuals have in common is the importance of defining aspirations.

Recognition for a job well done is the top motivator for employee performance.

Whenever a car dealership's service department is not open at least some hours on nights and weekends, I know the dealership doesn't care a shred about customer service.

Asking those who are involved in a life of chaos to be respectful of your time is like catching flies with chopsticks.

All plans need foundations, and the foundations are simple truths.

I'm all for working hard, damn hard, but there's something wrong, damn wrong, with people that always look frantic and preoccupied at the office.

You can't climb the ladder of success without first getting on the ladder.

Good news: every year, every week, even every day, we get to begin our world all over again.

Repetition is a prerequisite for change and success.

Great leaders aren't afraid of great conflicts.

❧

Hard work vaccinates against both boredom and poverty.

❧

Don't forget that Edison invented the lightbulb on roughly his ten thousandth attempt.

❧

At one time in our history, the model was: human beings walk, birds fly. The Wright Brothers ignored the model.

❧

Creative solutions can only arise from failures.

❧

The true goal of running a company is to make venture-taking feasible. Management cannot force its employees to be inventive — it can only furnish circumstances under which ingenuity thrives.

❧

Sitting through some unproductive business meetings feels is as uncomfortable as wearing shoes a size too small.

❧

The most important factor in deciding if a society will succeed is the ethics of the civilians, not the actions of the leaders.

❧

Truck drivers' wages aren't very high when there are no trucks around to drive.

❧

The biggest mistake people make when it comes to saving for retirement is thinking they don't have to do it on their own.

❦

There's a big difference between a job and a career.

❦

Most people are not idealogues — they are attracted to what works.

❦

As a leader, you must constantly change the definition of winning. Keep moving the goal posts.

❦

Most people I know have a heart, a mind, and, hopefully, a conscience. So, presumably, should the companies they work for.

❦

In business negotiations, I assume the best of the person I'm disagreeing with.

❦

To some degree, you control your life by controlling your time.

❦

I believe that people who work twelve hours a day should go home with bigger loaves of bread than people who work eight.

❦

We are all salespeople.

❦

When you think you've gotten something for nothing, you just haven't received the bill yet.

❦

Imagine applying for your current job. This exercise can stir up innovative thoughts about your work and how you do it.

❦

The only job security in the world is to be more talented tomorrow than you are today.

❦

Every leader of every corporation ought to go out and get a couple of the best books on psychology and read them.

❦

The divine mission of very large companies is simple but not easy: to instill in themselves the heart and soul of a small company.

❦

If your work doesn't provide the opportunity for spiritual, personal, and financial growth, you're spending far too much of your life on it.

❦

I love the idea of people bartering goods and services without cash. I don't understand why more people don't do it.

❦

Doctors that make you wait more than a half an hour to be seen without an explanation should be sent a bill for your wasted time.

❦

In terms of choosing a career, the trick is to find a job that you would do for free if life afforded you that opportunity.

❦

We're reaching a point in America where the value of time is beginning to equal to the value of money.

❦

I've observed that people like free markets as long as the economy is booming. As soon as the inevitable fluctuations occur, everyone complains bitterly and expects the government to step in immediately and remedy things. So, people want the energy and success of capitalism, but the safety of socialism. An impossible wish.

❦

One of the rules for success in the workplace is to show up 10 percent earlier than the appointed time and stay 10 percent after the closing time.

❦

Governing a company is like tending a garden — from time to time you need to just get out there and do some weeding.

❦

Nothing vaccinates against anarchy like a well-structured schedule.

❦

Lying fallow or chasing one's tail does to the human being exactly what I suspected — brings them down. Doers are happier than non-doers. Period.

❦

I don't know of any public figure who will not brag about having been poor in their youth. They wear their rags-to-riches stories like a Congressional Medal of Honor. With each telling, the road to school gets longer and bumpier, the temperature drops significantly and their

*lunchbox gets a little emptier. Overcoming adversity is the one thing
Americans can resist.*

✦

Many self-made men worship their creator.

✦

*We are making progress. Let's not forget that smallpox, cholera and
tuberculosis have been virtually eliminated.*

✦

In the final analysis, we are our choices.

✦

*When I think of the position taken by some of the academic elite, it
reminds me of the sad song, "Send in the Clowns". . . "don't bother,
they're here."*

✦

Rather than ask what makes nations poor, the more practical
approach is to look at what makes them rich.

✦

Even Chinese communists know the power of incentives.

✦

*Feeling omniscient, brilliant people can destroy themselves
by ignoring risks.*

✦

Relaxing is most necessary when you don't have time for it.

✦

Once upon a time, fame was the result of achievement.

✦

People with winning attitudes win.

❦

There doesn't seem to be any excuse for not giving to charity. None. If you can't afford even a small amount of money, then give your time.

❦

Isn't the definition of a genius someone who's done some Herculean pushing against the current wisdom that says "you can't do that"?

❦

Liberation means having choices; wisdom means understanding the costs.

❦

You can worry yourself to death.

❦

Boredom is the shriek of our unused capacity.

❦

Some people struggle harder to avoid health and sanity than a fish caught on dry land.

❦

Being able to vote is no more realizing freedom than being able to read is realizing wisdom.

❦

Attitude is the mother of luck.

❦

Relearning is harder than learning.

❦

Turning down the noise in your mind is an acquired skill.

꩜

Remember, underneath people's exquisite explanations for their problems with food, drugs, or alcohol are far deeper problems for which these symptoms only manifest.

꩜

I was fascinated to read in the British Medical Journal that department store mannequins are so skinny that they probably wouldn't have enough fat on them to menstruate if they were alive. The brainwash continues.

꩜

To constantly yield to instinctual urges is to give no thought to their consequences. To suppress them is to place too great a weight on them, thus enabling them to rule your life. The key, then, is to find some happy middle ground wherein lies both the knowledge of possible consequences and the power of moderation.

꩜

Isolation only magnifies your worries. Helping others will give you a sense of accomplishment and self-respect and remind you that, relatively speaking, your own troubles don't amount to a hill of beans in the world.

꩜

Have you ever counted up the number of times the word "genius" is used on award shows in Hollywood? And if all those people are geniuses, what was Einstein?

꩜

The intellectual elites of this country are not only out of touch with mainstream America, but they are violently contemptuous of it.

❦

There is a big difference between being smart and being wise. You can have a very quick mind, which is a good working definition for smart, but act very foolishly. A wise person is much rarer.

❦

Some ideas are really so stupid that only intellectuals could believe them.

❦

Ideas without plans are like snow in a hot oven.

❦

Logical consequences are invisible to fools and blinking neon to the wise.

❦

Wisdom is the quality that keeps you from getting into situations where you need it.

❦

Occasionally, the best answer to a question is a question.

❦

Today, instead of a plan, hope, or dream, everyone seems to have a scheme.

❦

Does anyone doubt that the mentally ill are victims not of weak character, but of bad chemistry?

❦

Building a business is much like building a house. It's much easier when you have a blueprint.

❦

Studies have shown that certain kinds of men will die almost immediately after their retirement. This is evidence that work-centered males suffer deeply, when stripped of their life's meaning.

❦

If most men spent as much time and attention on their personal financial matters as they do on ball scores, they would find retirement a lot easier.

❦

Self-made, wealthy accumulators spend far less than they can afford to on houses, cars, vacations, entertainment, etc. Why? Because these things offer little or no financial return. They would rather put their money into investments or their business, so their wealth grows.

❦

I miss the simpler days when fitness equipment was a machine consisting of a wide, rubber belt attached to a vibrating motor which operated on the principle that if you could shake up your fat in a rhythmic fashion, you could fool it into thinking it had been for a run.

❦

Life costs more than you expect.

❦

Grace

under Fire...

Now, whenever I order eggs, I think of my brain on drugs.

☞

The demise of those complicated, cold voice mail systems that large companies use would make me rejoice like the Munchkins did when they heard the Wicked Witch was dead.

☞

I love clever notes of complaint. My favorite to date is from a friend who protested the excess of his dental bill by writing, "Root canal? You charged me for the Suez Canal!" Don't you love it?

☞

Shaving on weekends is hateful.

☞

I can't help but think my car runs better after it's been freshly washed.

☞

I find myself more interested in talking to people who think about where the rain goes after it falls outside our windows than people who've taken the time to memorize their driver's license numbers.

❦

When all is said and done, I believe I'm happiest when I'm absorbed in fulfilling tasks, swept away by a sense of purpose.

❦

What I never expect to hear from my auto mechanic: "Oh, it was just a little loose wire. No charge."

❦

When I read most people's New Year's resolutions, I know they leave me feeling like the party is over.

❦

People I'd like to smack: junk mail senders, crank callers, loud neighbors, aggressive beggars, and telemarketers.

❦

Things I want to do before I die: 1. Have a love affair in Paris 2. Spend a whole day eating everything I have been told is bad for me 3. Be an extra in a film 4. Learn how to take a compliment 5. Send a message in a bottle 6. Swim with a dolphin 7. Plant a tree 8. Experience weightlessness 9. Forgive my parents and 10. Learn to handle tax forms, telephone solicitors, pushy Mormon missionaries, and power drills.

❦

I'd seriously rather stick a hot butter knife in my eye than go to an after-Christmas sale.

❦

Life is a great teacher. I learned that recently while pushing someone larger than me while playing basketball.

Life has taught me to examine the things I am the most sure of.

There are times I've been so scared I was sure the whole world could hear my heart pounding.

I'm frustrated that Adolph Hitler saved us the trouble by taking his own life.

I don't own a single thing made of Gortex — and I'm proud of it.

I'm finding myself increasingly bored with people who are bored. With so much to do in this world, why are so many people walking around looking like they just finished seeing two hundred slides of their neighbor's three-week vacation in Cleveland?

Some days for no perceptible reason I feel broken, lonely, scared, confused, hopeless, and more. I wonder if other people feel this way too. I seldom ask. After a good night's sleep or a talk with someone who holds my hand, kisses my forehead, and tells me to keep going, I'm usually just fine.

Some days when I have the distinct feeling I'm running up the down escalator, I must remember to turn around.

❦

I simply have not been able to find a way of being in a bad mood whenever I hear "Rhapsody in Blue."

❦

The weirdest dream I ever had involved being stuck in an elevator with Shari Lewis and Lambchop.

❦

What I never expected to hear from my dentist: "I think the problem is that you're flossing too much."

❦

Even though I want to do things in my life that will change the world, I find myself dreadfully shy about telling that to strangers.

❦

When someone who works for me is in a bad mood, I try to remember to buy them a pack of gum at lunch. More than half the time it makes their bad mood disappear.

❦

One night, to relieve some tension, I drew up a list of people I'd kill if they weren't already dead.

❦

The smell of incense makes me gag.

❦

I confess that I still place a great deal of emphasis on appearance even though I've run across a few well-dressed idiots.

❦

I love receiving personal letters form friends. Even thogh my life is filled with activity, personal letters provide momenatry escape, and I come back from them with a sense of renewed contentment.

❦

When I learn that a friend has lost their job, I call or drop a note asking if I can help in any way. I figure that for ten minutes of time, I might restore a person's faith in humanity.

❦

I only believe in forgiveness for people who say they're sorry. I don't believe in forgiving people who are not apologetic for what they did. If they're not regretful, it makes a mockery of the concept of forgiveness, not to mention justice.

❦

What I never expected to hear from a waiter: "Sir, I'm sorry. I was slow and inattentive and I cannot accept any tip."

❦

On a river rafting trip several years ago, I came to understand that the river doesn't stop. If you don't make a decision, it will make one for you.

❦

The things I'm grateful for: Not getting audited by the IRS, books on tape, Hitler didn't have the bomb, birth control, and seven-layer cake.

❦

The best advice that anyone's given me this year: Relax.

❦

Temptations I can't resist: To play "Heart and Soul" whenever I pass a piano. To put seashells to my ear even though I've never heard the sound of the ocean in one. To look up my last name in a telephone directory when I'm in a strange city.

Not everything that promises to contribute to happiness does.

Criticism to those you love should be rendered softly.

When you make a good-sized mistake, it's a good idea to write down what you've learned from it before a week passes. The process of wiring it and reading it again can help avoid repetition of it.

To ensure time to think, reflect, and ponder, schedule meetings with yourself and honor them as you would an appointment with another.

Beware of ideas that spring forth from people with too much time on their hands.

To learn more about who you are, try to describe yourself in three adjectives.

Stand tall. If you slouch, others will see you as lacking confidence, regardless of your other abilities.

As best you can, stop fighting with idiots.

❦

Make an audiotape of a conversation to hear how you sound to
other people. You'll be surprised.

❦

*Don't let your schedule determine your priorities. Make your priorities
determine your schedule.*

❦

The kind of exit you make is important if you're thinking
of coming back.

❦

Beware of coffee so strong that it will keep you up after you die.

❦

Never declare something unacceptable unless you have the
means to enforce its unacceptability.

❦

Pay more attention to your potential than to your history.

❦

Waking up an hour earlier each work day will give you an extra
month a year.

❦

*The trick to making yourself feel more secure in your life is making
insecurity your friend.*

❦

New Year's Day is a good day to look backwards and forwards.

❦

Finish your holiday shopping before Thanksgiving. Trust me.

❦

Don't board a ship when you don't know where it's going.

❦

Don't ask a question if you're not ready for the answer.

❦

You can help build a sense of community by taking time to learn the name of your local merchants and their employees, in addition to the folks that live next door to you.

❦

Aim to go where the action is going to be, not where it is.

❦

Decide early in any situation exactly what your bottom line is, then stick to it.

❦

Stick with what got you to the dance in the first place.

❦

People can accept sacrifice only when it's shared. No one loves a martyr.

❦

Fill the medicine cabinet before you get sick.

❦

Beware of people who spend a lot of time in tanning booths.

❦

Learn as if you'll live forever; live as if you'll die tomorrow.

❦

Whenever possible, wage one war at a time.

꩜

We need to spend less time worrying about the future and more time creating it.

꩜

If you want to sleep good, act good.

꩜

Two things that need to be changed in America: the emphasis we put on sports and way we treat the elderly. Two things that should not change: the taste of a Dove Bar and the colors in a crayon box.

꩜

Be wary of people who you have never heard say, "I'm sorry. I was wrong. I won't do it again."

꩜

In this age of self-involvement, people would be wise to place people intentionally in their life that are calculated to keep them humble. Three good suggestions include family, a religious community, and a therapist. All of these can act as a smoke alarm for self-involvement.

꩜

Believe less of what people say and more of what they do.

꩜

Refuse to give to any charity that refuses to give you a breakdown of where its money goes.

꩜

As an exercise for cutting out wasted words in business memo writing, pretend you're sending your document via Western Union and are paying $1 a word.

🍸

If you've never played a really good practical joke on someone, get cooking.

🍸

Every so often, try remembering . . . it's your life!

🍸

There seems to be only one decent position to face life: frontally.

🍸

How about this for an inventive way of spending a solo lunch hour: Write a long, chatty letter to an elderly relative.

🍸

During each day, try to take a minute and look at life with a sense of awe, being grateful for your liver, your hands, and your invisible, incomprehensibly complex mind. Treat life with reverence a few minutes a day, and you will contribute to your spiritual awakening faster than through any metaphysical course.

🍸

If you count your blessings as opposed to your calories, you'll lose weight faster.

🍸

I've come to regard those friends who I only speak to when I contact them as not really friends.

🍸

Liars never trust anyone.

❦

Education that withholds irony is ultimately condescending.

❦

In the wake of the year 2000, we are impelled to look back . . . sum up . . . compare.

❦

Whenever I travel, I listen to the local talk radio shows. This experience has conviced me that there are two types of people in the world: those who have something to say and cannot say it, and those who have nothing to say and never stop talking.

❦

Master

piece Theater...

I wonder if the person who invented raisin toast died with
a sense of accomplishment. I hope so.

❦

Good manners are like traffic rules for society.

❦

Today's celebrities, however talented, have devalued the
currency of stardom. As Emerson suggested, "Every hero
becomes a bore at last." And the process today is swift.

❦

*In this age of unparalleled TV diversity, including cable mania
and videotapes, it seems we may have lost forever the sense of
shared experience we, as a nation, had when Elvis or the
Beatles were first on TV.*

❦

Sacred cows have a rough time in steak country.

❦

Those who refuse to condemn evil done by minorities by attempting to excuse their rage, exacerbate that situation.

❦

School districts have a perverse incentive not to succeed, because when children perform badly, the schools usually get more money based on the argument that it lacks funds.

❦

In large part, a group's own culture is a strong determinant of its economic and social fate.

❦

Though people are very hesitant to point out the good reasons behind obvious stereotypes, the danger of not noting them is far worse than identifying them.

❦

Melting pots sometimes feel like pressure cookers.

❦

Teaching right from wrong has more bearing on the culture's survival as teaching reading, writing, history, and science.

❦

If you don't personally get to know people from other racial, religious, or cultural groups, it's very easy to believe ugly things about them and make them frightening in your mind.

❦

It is not part of the American culture, especially citizens from Texas, to disparage one's accomplishments.

❦

In cities and suburbs across America, it seems that the begging business is booming.

❦

There is a large, growing hole in the moral ozone layer of our society.

❦

The concept of vulgarity is disappearing because it is the norm.

❦

No level of teaching can promote wisdom in a culture in which people spend so many hours luxuriating in the neolithic swamp of television.

❦

The hidden cost of crime is that it is forcing us to teach our children to be motivated by fear instead of desire for life.

❦

Junkies need to realize that it wasn't society or pushers that put the first needle in their arm.

❦

Overburdened airline employees have entered a realm of rudeness once reserved for New York cab drivers and Las Vegas maitre'ds.

❦

The speed of news has changed. When Lincoln was assassinated, it took nearly a week to get the word out.

❦

The closest many people get to philosophy is watching Andy Rooney complain on Sunday night.

❦

Style is a matter of timing.

❦

We live in an age where competence is perceived as excellence.

❦

Contemporary times demand too much of children and too little of adults.

❦

The goal should be to make Watts more like Beverly Hills and not Beverly Hills more like Watts.

❦

Loving people because of their race is just as bigoted as hating people because of their race.

❦

The more racial and ethnic pride you have, the less individual pride you have. The way to grow up is to see yourself as an individual first.

❦

Socialism is an extravagant historical failure because it runs contrary to human nature, by suppressing the individuals.

❦

Noting society's fascination with the bizarre, sensational, and criminal, one wonders if Hitler would be discovered to be alive, would his first stop be Nuremburg or Nightline?

❦

As long as we pay the poor to continue doing the very things that make them poor in the first place, poor they shall remain.

❦

The hopelessness of poverty is not seen as vividly through the serenity of the air-conditioned, urbane halls of Yale as they are to those who have become anaesthetized to the common smell of urine.

In general, we've replaced the noble concept of the hero with the thin veneer of fame.

The once scholarly craft of biography writing has frequently mutated into a scramble for scandal.

Many African-Americans are so instinctively distrustful of white society that they automatically reject any idea or judgment the origins of which are not easily traced to their community.

We've become a more cautious world, one in which most people don't want to "inhale."

Research confirms that low- to moderate-income people are more generous than upper income people, contributing volunteer time and money to help the needy and minority groups. It is ironic and depressing, but not especially surprising.

Just because something is silly doesn't mean it isn't also dangerous.

When your life is bereft of passion and excitement, you start searching it out, desparately everywhere.

Organizations that refuse to criticize themselves lose credit at the bar of public opinion and should be ultimately dismissed as cultist.

❦

Far more often than poverty breeds crime, crime breeds poverty.

❦

The reason crime rates are surging is that, for many people, the benefits of crime far outweigh the costs.

❦

How about this as an antigang program: Let's mandate that all apprehended thugs must witness a gang member's postmortem examination, as a way of teaching how to respect others' lives. One visit to the coroner's office should do it.

❦

I think the time has come to augment the Statue of Liberty on the East Coast with a Statue of Responsibility on the West Coast. Why? Because it's time to promote human responsibility. Nowadays, emphasis has been placed almost exclusively on the rights of the individual. Without acknowledging our obligations to society.

❦

It's important to remember that culture wars always precede shooting wars.

❦

Our fast-paced modern world is suffering from a reverence famine.

❦

Trying to identify who the moderates are in the Middle East is like trying to identify who is the smartest of the Three Stooges.

❦

Americans have a fascination with games of chance, including marriage and politics.

❦

I don't know about you, but I get the feeling that most media in this country are on a search to show that the unconventional is the norm and have unlimited capacity to find experts somewhere who will say just about anything, especially if it seems to make no common sense.

❦

The volume of the chorus of self-proclaimed victims in our nation has become so high and shrill that if Walt Whitman were to come back he wouldn't hear America singing. He would hear America whining.

❦

Aren't you a little embarrassed to live in the most economically comfortable time and place in history and not be happy?

❦

Estimating the true cost of violent crime is probably impossible. Beyond the financial losses, how do we calculate the psychic and spiritual damage done by torturers, murderers, and rapists?

❦

Be patient with yourself. Remember, it took you a lifetime to become how you are at this moment.

❦

Isn't taxing ammunition to pay for some health care an idea that's worth considering?

❦

When you think about it, even for a little while, it is easy to understand why people join cults. They weld members into a social unit so that they can feel they belong and share their private craziness with others in a form of socially accepted insanity. Their unreality is valid because many others believe it; and the more who believe, the more who are reassured and relieved not to be alone.

❧

This is an age of facts — not knowledge, not cleverness, not wisdom.

❧

When pornography was defined as appealing exclusively to the prurient interests and having no "redeeming social importance," didn't it take into account that the prurient can be of social importance?

❧

While people receive more schooling than ever, they don't seem better educated.

❧

From time to time, ask yourself the question, "What are you clinging to?"

❧

Noting the beauty of Shakespeare's letters, I wonder what would have happened if he had used the phone.

❧

Why is the computer system I bought a few years ago now worth less than the coffee maker I bought in the early 1970s?

❧

Why does Perry Como always look so damn relaxed?

❦

Does it seem that suffering makes most people contemplate, and that reflection makes people astute, and that knowledge makes the existence possible?

❦

Most people are afraid that if anyone saw the truth about them they would be turned off and run the other way. Not so. Truth is more appealing than deceit.

❦

If television and movie violence is responsible for real-life atrocities, then is Walt Disney responsible for any deer killed in a similar manner to Bambi's mother?

❦

Have you ever stolen a towel from a hotel? Did you want to give it back? This brings up a whole hotel morality, you know. How far should you go? For example, you are certainly entitled to take a few pieces of hotel stationary. But should you take the pen?

❦

How did we get to the point where everyone is a victim?

❦

I agree that we don't spend enough money on AIDS research, but how much would be enough?

❦

Why do dentists insist on asking questions after they put their hands in your mouth?

❦

In our effort to be gentle with our words, we mustn't forget that people who lie are called liars.

❦

Is there anything worse than an insincere smile?

❦

Doesn't a minute seem like an hour when you're waiting outside a bathroom door?

❦

Question to God: Why did you give men genitals if you wanted them to think clearly?

❦

Some things, which aren't, look so good on paper.

❦

Gossip is the only thing that travels faster than E-mail.

❦

Because most people's sex lives are so relatively tame, they long for a cauldron of steamy sexuality in their movies, music and media.

❦

The most ruthless dictator's power is not as great as a typical parents' power over a child.

❦

Those who define their race as a supreme fact of life, have moved very far from Martin Luther King's dream in which color made no difference.

❦

The renowned biblical saying about wealth is not about wealth, but about being addicted to it. It is the addiction to wealth that is the root of all evil, not wealth itself.

❦

Watching dayime talk shows is a powerful commercial against the human species. I don't know of any place where they so colorfully try to turn us into brutes and make us long to go on all fours.

❦

I've grown endlessly bored with those chronic ingrates that review our society the way pigeons review statues.

❦

Equal

Justice...

Repay kindness with kindness, but repay evil with justice.

🍇

Wealthy Americans who call our economic system "despicable" are merely political bulemics. After having eaten ravenoulsy at our table, they put their fingers down their throats to vomit at the banquet.

🍇

Most legal suits end up in compromise on the courthouse steps.

🍇

If it's true that a drowning person sees their whole life flash before them as they sink for the third time? Then what's happening to the criminal justice system is having the same effect on me.

🍇

There aren't always two sides to every story.

🍇

Lawyers understand that you win some and you lose some, but you get paid for all of them.

❦

When you under-punish criminals, you punish the innocent.

❦

Murderous dictators inherited their ethics from nature.

❦

Why is it that the more shocking the criminal act, the more difficult it is to prosecute?

❦

Beware of literal interpretations. "An eye for an eye and a tooth for a tooth" has little to with the subject of either optometry or dentistry.

❦

You cannot pardon somebody for a crime they have not committed.

❦

Beware of those who use litigation to repair the natural pain of life.

❦

Neighborhoods unravel when small infractions go unpunished.

❦

We need to recognize the reality of difference in our quest for equality.

❦

Murderers thrive in a country where there are over 20,000 homicides annually and about thirty executions.

❦

I thought about it a fair amount and don't think it's fair that U.S. citizenship should be automatically granted to children born to people that have broken laws by entering our country illegally.

❦

Remember, Manson thinks the police are nuts.

❦

For a police officer, a good day is a boring day.

❦

The best defense is often a brazen offense.

❦

On the question of immigration, it's becoming harder to decide who is the victim of political persecution and who is an economic gate-crasher.

❦

Certain political and social radicals are as annoying and noisy as a nickel in a dryer.

❦

No doubt, the Great Depression was a powerful experience for everyone it touched. But few realize how much it changed the government forever. After all, it was the Depression that created the fear of job loss, which created an activist federal government inextricably involved in the everyday lives of ordinary Americans. And so, what we wanted is now what we dread.

❦

We cannot help the economy without the rich getting richer.

❦

Never forget — terrorists hate democracy.

❦

Unrestricted illegal immigration is a time bomb.

᳅

City officials should wander through their city to get a feel for what is going on, just like corporate heads should wander through their company.

᳅

So that politicians can really and truly understand the public wrath at bureaucrats, I suggest they stand in line at the Department of Motor Vehicles office in any major city in this country. After that, they'll get it.

᳅

In politics, a quick, offensive commercial is equal to hundred blue-ribbon-panel status papers.

᳅

It is fascinating that many of the earth's dictators, who rule so mercilessly at home, speak so generously at the United Nations about the poor and downtrodden of the world.

᳅

I'm not sure that people who say religion and politics don't mix understand either.

᳅

Important historical documents are worth looking at every so often.

᳅

It's no secret that politicians have a unique skill of disconnecting themselves from the world of concrete, practical reality. In an individual, this would be called mental illness.

I find myself attracted to those in politics who promise the least. It seems to be a good way of controlling my disappointment.

"Oh God" is most people's reaction to long-term politicians who talk about problems they helped create, like preachers talking about fornication.

Every country is prepared to volunteer another country's army.

After decades of failure, social engineers have neither been discouraged nor discredited in trying to replace what works with what sounds good.

How about ten lashes as punishment for those who stand convicted of helping fillet common sense from political dialogue in the name of good motives.

Remember that the bureaucrats that create regulatory Hell for businesses are often not evil people, they're worse. They're people with good intentions and little understanding. At the root of their action is the belief in government as Santa Claus, who gives things away at no cost to anyone.

Our society stands perched above deeply embedded values and standards, against which nihilists have railed, not always in vain.

❦

Popularity in politics is a temporary window, with an opportunity for leaders to act boldly.

❦

A growth in the federal budget is by no means an indicator of growth in society's compassion.

❦

The process of government is slower than a tractor being towed out of an avalanche.

❦

At some point we are going to have to confront the reality that Vietnam is a country, not a war.

❦

Bad policies are often simply good policies carried too far.

❦

We cannot give strength to the powerless by taking it away from those with strength.

❦

Temporary political policies seem to last the longest.

❦

A group should be judged by the way its leaders deal with corruption, not by the depravity inside of it.

❦

No amount of reading or conversation on the subject of violence has put things in perspective for me as well as counting to twelve and realizing that another woman has been beaten by her spouse, lover, or ex.

The government should be problem-solving's last resort.

Simply accepting those of different creeds and colors is not enough. It is our responsibility to glorify diversity.

Beyond a certain point, public pressure tends to produce the opposite of what was intended.

The worst wars are civil.

Americans are so dissatisfied with politics, in large part, that it will be hard to restore faith unless government leaders stop repeatedly making commitments that can't be kept. However, I believe, there is a large constituency for candor.

Don't you wish that politicians would have the guts not to listen to the loudest, most militant voices but instead, to listen to average citizens with the more sensible views?

I like the Australian idea of naming hurricanes after unpopular politicians.

The struggle for power is the essence of history. The battle between those holding power and the have-nots.

❦

Perhaps the only good thing gained from wealthy people running for political offices is that most people take care of what they pay for.

❦

I define leaders as people who are willing to do the right thing. What we have in abundance in this country are people who do things right. It is this exchange of imagination for pragmatism that bothers me most.

❦

One of Washington's eternal truths is that "a government that robs Peter to pay Paul is guaranteed to get Paul's vote in the next election."

❦

Politicians love talking about "socking it to the rich." However, I wonder if the real purpose of making the rich scream is to obscure the sound of the middle class getting mugged.

❦

In politics, it matters not if a policy is popular, but whether its effects will be popular.

❦

Vigorous questioning can propel a restoration and deepening of conviction. Skepticism is a phase, not an eternal condition; out of the embryo of uncertainty grows the examination that produces a deeper,

*common, more genuine conviction. Paradoxically, it is the very
questioning that causes the rubbing that polishes the pearl.*

❦

In political affairs, not to mention many personal situations, it
seems that once you permit a rogue to survive, you often face
endless challenges and crises.

❦

*As a way of getting government spending under control, why don't we
add up all the government spending that a Congressional
representative votes for in the course of the year and assess taxpayers
in the district accordingly?*

❦

Knowing what you know now, if we were in the midst of the
Vietnam war and you were drafted, would you serve?

❦

*I don't believe any politician opposed to the death penalty can ever be
elected president, no matter how brilliant or charismatic they were in
every other issue. In the gut of most Americans there is the feeling that
anyone who wants to let murderers live has a moral screw loose.*

❦

In solving our abominable deficit problem, we must adopt a
legendary Noah principle: No more prizes for predicting rain.
Prizes only for building arks.

❦

*Noting the selection of candidates we're generally given, Halloween is
not nearly as scary as Election Day.*

❦

Maybe the reason that Congressional representatives try so hard to get reelected is that they would hate to have to try to earn a living under the laws that they've passed.

🎐

I don't think anything makes my blood get hotter or my brow wetter than the idea that there are actually legislators that recommend releasing murderers back into society. According to my law, they should be locked up alongside their vicious friends.

🎐

Someone wise once said that "a man may be a very good Christian and a bad Chancellor of Exchequer." That principle has me restlessly thinking about whether I prefer to be governed by an adulterer with a sound anti-inflationary view or by a Socialist monk.

🎐

Why is it that today, concepts that should be obvious seem obscure: Government debt is bad and leads to instability and inflation; savings and personal responsibility are the foundations of individual and national security; and moving away from these principles leads to disaster.

🎐

I don't think anyone would have been more amused by the sentimental myth of Camelot imposed upon the presidency of John F. Kennedy after his death than the martyred hero himself.

🎐

*The quickest route to oppression is the reckless
application of independence.*

❧

The appropriate reaction to people who hurt themselves is pity;
and to those that hurt others, contempt.

❧

The evening news has become a police blotter.

❧

Governments have great power to reward or penalize various
behavior, and misguided policies can be fatal.

❧

*If "pro" is the opposite of "con", isn't it obvious what the opposite
of progress is¿*

❧

While the equality of opportunity is a reasonable goal, the
quality of outcome is impossible.

❧

Truth is often determined by context.

❧

The trouble with lawyers jokes is lawyers don't think they're
funny and nobody else thinks they're jokes.

❧

*Reporters and voters are like horses and dogs; they can sense when
someone is fearful.*

❧

Lawyers delight in the inconsistency of laws and hence try and write them in a desecratory manner. Therefore, they have the incentive to legislate.

🌱

How many marriages would you expect to see if the government started giving away engagement rings?

🌱

In the courtroom today, "beyond a reasonable doubt" has been superseded by "beyond any shred of an excuser."

🌱

Liberals believe that conservatives are corrupt and conservatives believe liberals are fools.

🌱

It's better to die on your feet than to live on your knees.

🌱

Abortion touches on three of the world's most contentious subjects — religion, sex and politics.

🌱

Blessed are politicians who get to the point of a difficult question with carrier-pigeon directness.

🌱

While it may be legally wrong for a government to subsidize a particular political movement at the expense of others, it isn't always morally wrong.

🌱

In terms of trust, most attorneys hold a place in the public mind somewhere between a loan shark and a communist spy.

※

I've always believed that a thriving democracy derives its strength and character from the diversity of its many voices. But that's not what our government is. After all, there aren't a whole lot of plumbers or scientists in government. In fact, there seems to be but one voice — that of a full-time politician who is almost always a lawyer.

※

Politics seems to be one of the few places left where one can demonstrate ignorance and execrable judgment and, yet get a promotion.

※

Leap

# of Faith...

More and more it seems the faithful distort God's message and hear, "Love thy neighbor, hate thyself."

🌱

The word "charisma" was derived from an expression meaning "of the spirit or inspired."

🌱

While most contemporary people think of sin as an outmoded idea, it is very much alive and more deadly than ever. Greed, envy, lust, pride, anger, sloth, and gluttony cause as much unhappiness today as in any time in history.

🌱

To have faith requires courage.

🌱

The size of airline seats is the definition of Hell itself.

🌱

In forming one's belief system, a person has to finally, often painfully, reach an answer to the question of whether God is necessary or not for morality.

Today you can post the Ten Commandments in Moscow public schools, but it's illegal to do it in the United States.

Sadly, there are those that live in such a religiously isolated world that they don't even come into contact with those in their own religion who hold different views.

People who proselytize their religious doctrine should contain themselves to speaking when invited and stopping when asked. Otherwise, a sock of manure seems appropriate.

Most everyone turns to God in anguish.

Remember, there's a profound difference between God allowing something to happen and God willing something to happen.

Churchgoers should remember that they are there to worship God, not the church.

I think Dante was right: the final circle of Hell is reserved for perpetrators of betrayal.

When you get unduly angry, sin is crouching at the door.

❧

The self-righteous are afflicted by their gift for justifying everything, whereas the rest of us must simply face the truth.

❧

Those who are cruel to others will live lives
of ultimate self-abuse.

❧

Without reason, blind faith becomes a scourge.

❧

The ultimate goal is not to escape from the brutality of this
world into the clandestine presence of God.

❧

Holiness is gained by our actions. Not by simply entering a sanctuary.

❧

The power of the priest in the past has transferred
to the psychiatrist.

❧

It's interesting to remember that the Pope's boss is a Jewish carpenter.

❧

The sixth Commandment is "thou shalt not murder," not "kill."
A big difference.

❧

In a restless heart, the seeds of betrayal lie.

❧

Today, before the sun sets, chances are an angel will
pass your way.

❦

The sign outside the gates of salvation says, "Be grateful."

❦

Believing in God is not as difficult as loving God in this world
of unjust suffering.

❦

*When you pray for the trivial like, say, a sports team winning, you
have confused God with Santa Claus.*

❦

The danger is not in believing in God, but in believing God to
be on your side.

❦

*Simply saying prayers is not praying, otherwise, a team of properly
trained parrots would be guaranteed heaven.*

❦

Some people involve themselves in religion as an opportunity
to approach mystery, and other people go into religion
to escape mystery.

❦

*Religion doesn't guarantee goodness, but the death of
religion guarantees evil.*

❦

We cannot fully live until there is something that we are willing
to die for.

❦

Most of us know someone who is pathetically obsessed by their religious beliefs. They in fact make God a drug and set up their church as the absolute authority of all aspects of life. They don't ask questions, think for themselves, or doubt their church at all. They follow the church blindly and obey without question.

Our fascination with the mystical is largely the result of the failure of secular substitutes to give satisfying answers to the truly significant puzzles in life: evil, goodness, suffering, love, death, and the meaning of it all.

"Acts of God" like tornadoes, earthquakes, and floods, which may kill and maim one family and leave their neighbors untouched, raise the unanswerable question of God's role in unjust suffering.

If it is not possible for you believe in miracles, then it is not possible for you to believe in God.

If secular critics in the media holds up Jimmy Swaggart's deviant lechery as proof of the horrors of religion, why don't they ever mention the lack of regular church or synagogue attendance by the gang on death row?

In response to people who exclaim to me that "God is love!" I remind them that God is also truth, justice, punishment, and law.

After attending a funeral, I remember thinking that places of death are important schools for the living.

❦

Clergy that go out of their way to shun sinners are similar to doctors who treat only healthy people.

❦

If you really believe that God is all-knowing, all-powerful, and all-good, then worrying about things that are out of your control is a subtle form of atheism.

❦

My experience with rigid religions leads me to ask the following question: How much of the attraction is theological and how much is that they present a very tight-knit, structured, and family-like environment in an age of chaos and confusion, providing members with either a family they never had or are desperately afraid to leave? The former provides an explanation for conversion, and the latter insight to keeping their world tightly sealed. Understanding this motivation is critical. Mark Twain wisely pointed out, "When a person cannot deceive himself, the chances are against them being able to deceive other people." Evil people never ask themselves, "Am I evil?"

❦

The only place where people are entirely guilt-free is prison.

❦

Often, criminals have made a rational decision to be criminals.

❦

Morality demands knowing that some things are right and others are wrong.

❦

What needs more exploration is not why some people are criminals, but why most people are not.

❦

There are only two races in the world: the decent and the indecent.

❦

Frauds reveal themselves under stress.

❦

It is interesting to note that what categorizes mass murderers most profoundly is the conviction that they've been wronged by a hostile world. What's missing is any sense that they might be at fault.

❦

The human is tireless in attempting to find psychological and sociological reasons to excuse the behavior that our minds won't accept as Evil.

❦

Bigoted church folk are often more vulgar than bigoted atheists.

❦

Blessed are those who answer simple questions directly and laconically.

❦

Don't magnify your monsters. Remember, Dorothy simply threw water on the Wicked Witch and, poof! — she was vanquished.

❦

Powerful people often lose touch with the real world, believing that society's regulations don't apply. They become conditioned to believe that others will understand their actions based on their accomplishments.

❧

Successful people often like to see how much they can get away with, much like teenagers testing their parents.

❧

There are gradations of evil.

❧

The consequence to the belief that there are no bad people is that there are no good people.

❧

Only the victim can ultimately forgive the perpetrator of a crime.

❧

Champions keep their commitments.

❧

Are moral muscles like regular muscles? Do they atrophy if they're not exercised? Is it possible that without practice and self-discipline, anyone can turn into something of a dissolute?

❧

Young children (and most Hollywood agents) make moral decisions based on "what's in it for me?" logic.

❧

If E.T. landed in your backyard, would you bring him into your home and feed him, or try to kill him?

❧

The great religious texts throughout the ages wouldn't always be exhorting us to do good if they didn't recognize that we're inclined, so often, to do evil.

❧

People who lie frequently (to others and to themselves) ultimately get good at it, and usually arrive at a level of exquisite adroitness.

❧

Good people don't realize how bad bad people are.

❧

180 degrees from wrong is still wrong.

❧

People who start cheating at solitaire end up cheating at bridge.

❧

Many people think they are good simply because they desist from doing bad. They are wrong. They are not good, they are just not bad.

❧

With the same assuredness that I am convinced that God wants us to be good, I am equally sure that God doesn't want us to be stupid.

❧

There are obnoxious people who may be telling the truth, and there are charming people who may not be.

❧

The question asked by Confucius centuries ago may be among the most penetrating ever posed: "If we treat those who do bad good, how will we treat those who do good?"

❦

I trust we all know someone who we wouldn't be surprised to see walking down Lover's Lane holding their own hand.

❦

Anyone who starts by caring more for his own belief system than truth will advance by loving his own group better than goodness, and end by loving himself infinitely more than mankind.

❦

The question is often asked, "Why is there evil in the world?" Yet almost never asked is the question, "Why is there such good?" Noting that evil is far easier for the human to do than good, logic demands that the world is naturally more evil, and has been mysteriously injected with goodness.

❦

Nearly all criminals have the same theory of economic success: All wealth they feel, comes from stealing; successful Italian restaurants are fronts for the Mafia; successful actresses, models and businesswomen are all really whores. Oil tycoon John B. Rockefeller, one man says, made his fortune as a member of the Jesse James gang and founded Standard Oil as a front. Everyone steals. My informants were merely unlucky enough to get caught.

❦

The tongue is the part of the body that sins the most.

❦

I'm convinced that some liars really aim to tell the truth. They just have really bad aim.

❦

Cults are like a slime that oozes into the cracks of people's lives.

❦

The difference between the good and the great is inches and miles.

❦

We have a better understanding of our primitive evolution than our faith in divine creation.

❦

We are all mentors, menders, and missionaries.

❦

The older I get, the more heartfelt my prayers become.

❦

All of us are born for a reason, but all of us don't discover why.

❦

The deed shapes the heart more than the heart shapes the deed.

❦

Just because God cannot be proved rationally does not mean faith in him is irrational.

❦

Finishing some books is like saying goodbye to a dying friend.

❦

About the Author

Michael Levine turned forty on April 17, 1994.

George McGovern, *Former Senator and Presidential Candidate*

Michael Levine has discovered some invaluable lessons that can be helpful to the rest of us. Few observers can give us more intriguing and worthwhile lessons at the halfway point. You'll love this book . . . I did.

Michael Medved, *Film Critic*

Witty, thought-provoking, and occasionally even wise. It's the kind of book that's hard to stop reading once you've gotten started.

Prof. Wolfgang Mieder, *Proverb Scholar, Author*

From the point of view of a proverb scholar, I very much enjoyed the way you reacted to certain proverbial structures, sometimes agreeing with the traditional wisdom, sometimes also parodying it or putting a new twist on the traditional wisdom. It has long been my feeling that there is too little aphoristic writing in the United States, and I welcome your texts.

Thomas S. Monaghan, *Founder, Domino's Pizza, Inc.*

In his funny, subtle way, Michael Levine gives some good advice: "Take action!" There is too much potential out there, too many opportunities available for people to just sit back and ignore them. Action means results.

Prof. Linus Pauling, *Nobel Prize Winner*

A daring, deep exploration of the human experience. Endlessly thought-provoking.

Tom Peters, *Author* In Search of Excellence

I loved *Lessons at the Halfway Point.*

Regis Philbin, *Talk-Show Host*

It's all so true, it's scary . . . and funny too.

Dennis Prager, *Radio & Television Talk-Show Host*

Michael Levine's words have power and wisdom. They have truly moved me.

Dan Rather,
Anchor, CBS News

Am I at the halfway point yet? Have I learned anything? These are the kind of questions that put sweat on my brow. I'm awfully bad at coming up with lessons. It may be that I have too much respect for teachers to try and impart any lessons of my own.

Richard Rodriguez,
Author, Syndicated Columnist

America should declare Michael Levine the 51st state in the Union.

Dr. Jonas Salk,
Creator of the Polio Vaccine

It has been said that the unexamined life is not worth living. Michael Levine examines his with great wit and wisdom.

Rabbi Harold M. Sculweis, *Author,* For Those Who Can't Believe

Michael Levine has gifted the reader with aphorisms of wisdom, wit, and insight relevant to coping with the challenges of contemporary living.

Sidney Sheldon,
Author

Strong . . . clear . . . powerful. It makes you think and re-think. Filled with excitement , filled with passion, on the greatest adventure of all life.

Mother Theresa,
Winner of Nobel Peace Prize

Thank you for *Lessons*. Never think that a small action done to your neighbor is not worth much. It is not how much we do that is pleasing to God, but how much love we put into the doing. God bless you.

Dr. Denis Waitley,
Author, Empires of the Mind

Beyond Michael Levine's remarkable wit, is a laser-accurate, soul-deep wisdom incredibly perceptive for our times. He teaches us more at the halfway point than most of us learn over the entire journey!